Summary and Analysis of Atomic Habits:

An Easy and Proven Way to Build Good Habits and Break Bad Ones

by

James Clear

BOOK TIGERS

Note to readers:

This is an unofficial summary & analysis of James Clear, Atomic Habits: An Easy and Proven Way to Build Good Habits and Break Bad Ones, designed to enrich your reading experience.

Scan here to buy the original book.

Disclaimer: All Rights Reserved. No part of this publication may be reproduced or retransmitted, electronic or mechanical, without the written permission of the publisher; with the exception of brief quotes used in connection in reviews written for inclusion in a magazine or newspaper.

This book is licensed for your personal enjoyment only. This book may not be re-sold or given away to other people. If you would like to share this book with another person, please purchase an additional copy for each recipient. If you're reading this book and did not purchase it, or it was not purchased for your use only, then please purchase your copy.

Product names, logos, brands, and other trademarks featured or referred to within this publication are the property of their respective trademark holders. These trademark holders are not affiliated with us and they do not sponsor or endorse our publications. This book is unofficial and unauthorized. It is not authorized, approved, licensed, or endorsed by the aforementioned interests or any of their licensees.

The information in this book has been provided for educational and entertainment purposes only.

The information contained in this book has been compiled from sources deemed reliable and it is accurate to the best of the Author's knowledge; however, the Author cannot guarantee its accuracy and validity and cannot be held liable for any errors or omissions. Upon using the information contained in this book, you agree to hold harmless the author from and against any damages, costs, and expenses, including any legal fees, potentially resulting from the application of any of the information provided by this guide. The disclaimer applies to any damages or injury caused by the use and application, whether directly or indirectly, of any advice or information presented, whether for breach of contract, tort, neglect, personal injury, criminal intent, or under any other cause of action. You agree to accept all risks of using the information presented inside this book.

The fact that an individual or organization is referred to in this document as a citation or source of information does not imply that the author or publisher endorses the information that the individual or organization provided. This is an unofficial summary & analytical review and has not been approved by the original author of the book.

Download Your Free Gift

Before you go any further, why not pick up a gift from us to you?

Investing In You – Using the Power of Positive Thinking.

You will understand the true power of your positive thinking and subconscious mind and you will have absolute control over them, very fast!

Scan the QR code to get it before it expires!

Table of Contents

Book Summary Overview 7
Chapter by Chapter Analysis 8
Chapter 1 10
Chapter 2 14
Chapter 3 16
Chapter 4 18
Chapter 5 20
Chapter 6 22
Chapter 7 24
Chapter 8 26
Chapter 9 29
Chapter 10 31
Chapter 11 33
Chapter 12 35
Chapter 13 37
Chapter 14 39
Chapter 15 41
Chapter 16 43
Chapter 17 45
Chapter 18 47
Chapter 19 49
Chapter 20 51

Background Information about Atomic Habits 54
Background Information about James Clear 55
Cover Questions 56
Thank You 57
Download Your Free Gift 58
Discover the Book Tigers Series 59

Book Summary Overview

James Clear has divided his book *Atomic Habits: An Easy and Proven Way to Build Good Habits and Break Bad Ones* in 6 major parts. He lays the foundation of his novel model and explains its power in the first part. In the next four parts, he provides a comprehensive analysis of his 4 Laws of Behavior Change framework. An actionable, simple, and effective step-by-step process of changing your habits by designing your environment and taking advantage of how the human brain works. In the end, he offers advanced tactics to achieve your full potential and reach greatness. This is an overall highly actionable, science-based, and extremely versatile framework that can be applied to every aspect of life, from business to parenting. The book has a lot of extra resources to help the reader apply every instruction and their expanded versions are available for download on the author's site atomichabits.com.

Chapter by Chapter Analysis

*A*tomic Habits: An Easy and Proven Way to Build Good Habits and Break Bad Ones is the #1 New York bestseller book by James Clear, a pioneer on habit creation. Renowned authors Mark Manson (The Subtle Art of Not Giving A F*ck), Adam Grant (Originals), and Ryan Holiday (The Obstacle is The Way) refer to the value of this "revolutionary system to get 1 percent better every day" and the years James Clear has spent to hone the art and science of habits. The compound effect of hundreds of small decisions has a tremendous impact on the career, the relationships, and the life of the reader. The author calls those small decisions atomic habits.

The introduction of the book is written by the author, where he talks about his story. He had an accident in high school with a baseball bat that broke his nose, caused him multiple skull fractures, and two shattered eye sockets. When the nurse asked him some general questions, he was unable to answer any of them correctly. He was transferred via helicopter to the nearest, well-equipped hospital where he ended up spending the night in a medically induced coma and with several machines keeping him alive. Although he was released from the coma the next day, his left eye was bulged and had double vision for weeks.

It took eight months for the seizures to stop, have his eye in its normal location, and drive a car. His return to the baseball team wasn't smooth, either. He was rejected by the varsity team the first year he returned and the next year he barely played two games. However, it was in college that he learned the power of small habits and transformed his life. He started keeping his room neat, getting to bed early, and improving his study habits which resulted in him regaining confidence, earning straight A's, and getting better at sports. Four years into college and he managed to earn the President's Medal and be named to the ESPN Academic All-America-Team. Every single achievement, he attributes it to the compound effect of his small, but consistent habits, and none to overnight success.

In November 2012 Clear started publishing articles on his website twice a week. This single habit led to more than 30.000 subscribers by the end of 2013 and over 200.000 subscribers in 2015. At that point, he signed this book's deal, started delivering keynote speeches, and saw his articles published in Times, Forbes, and Entrepreneur. In 2017 he launched the Habits Academy, where he has trained since over 10.000 leaders, managers, coaches, and teachers.

In the final part of the introduction, the author offers some background for the book. He aimed to write an operating manual, an action-packed book backed by much scientific evidence. He introduces a four-step model of habits - cue, craving, response, and reward – and four laws of behavior change to create better habits. He offers "one of the first models of human behavior to accurately account for both the influence of external stimuli and internal emotions on our habits."

Chapter 1

The first part of the book "The Fundamentals: Why Tiny Changes Make a Big Difference" begins with chapter one, titled "The Surprising Power of Atomic Habits". The author recounts the incredible story of British Cycling and the strategy of its performance director Dave Brailsford. His idea was that if they improved every single part of cycling by 1%, "the aggregation of marginal gains" will result in a significant increase in performance. And he was right. The changes he issued - from redesigning the bike seat to hiring a doctor and teaching the athletes how to wash their hands – had British Cyclists winning 178 world championships, 66 gold medals, and 5 Tour de France victories.

The big difference that evolves from daily small habits and changes is represented by a single multiplication. The simple act of getting 1% better each day for one year equals to $1.01^{365}=37.78$ while getting worse 1% each day for a year equals to $0.99^{365}=0.03$. While a single decision (good or bad) doesn't produce a significant impact, the compound of small choices has an exponential effect. Thus it is more important to focus on the current trajectory than the current results. The outcomes are a lagging measure of current habits and time behaves as a multiplier of the effects of those habits. The author provides a table where he contrasts the long-term compounds of positive and negative habits.

Progress is not linear and, expecting it to be, makes sticking to a habit hard. Persisting to a good habit or resisting to a bad one, seems to have no significant or even noticeable effect for a long time, until it reaches a "breakthrough moment". That is the result of many previous actions that build up the potential required to unleash a major change. The author identifies the period of time that the stored effect grows over time as the "Plateau of Latent Potential". This "Valley of Disappointment" is where good habits die before their effect reaches the breakthrough point and is the time that great patience is required because the most powerful outcomes are delayed. All big things come from small beginnings. The seed of every habit is a single, tiny decision.

To overcome the Plateau of Latent Potential the author suggests to "Forget about Goals, Focus on Systems Instead". Setting specific and actionable goals is not enough, they are the desirable results. Goals offer a direction, but systems are about the progress towards those results. Designing successful systems means building habits to get better each day and, as someone who has won Super Bowl three times, Bill Walsh said that you don't have to focus on the score, because it will take care of itself.

Four specific problems occur when there is too much focus on the goal instead of designing a successful system. The first problem is that "Winners and losers have the same goal" and thus when we focus on winners, we assume that ambitious goals are the reason for their success. This survival bias can easily be countered by observing a little closer. All the participants in the Tour de France, for example, had the same goal, but the one with the best systems won.

The second problem is that achieving a goal, e.g. cleaning a messy room, is like treating a symptom. Yes, the room is cleaned, but the underlying cause, the habits that lead to a messy room, don't change requiring each time to achieve the goal anew.

The third problem is that goals restrict happiness by creating an "either-or" conflict. Being happy depends on whether the goal is achieved, instead of a mentality that allows satisfaction every time the system is running.

The final problem occurs when the goal is achieved and then there is no motivation to keep trying. Lack of commitment hinders long-term progress and leads to old, negative habits. A system comprised of little and healthy habits is a system of compound growth. Habits are like the atoms of our lives and the source of incredible power, that's why they are called atomic.

Are you enjoying the book so far?

If so, please help us reach more readers by taking 30 seconds to write just a few words on Amazon.

Or, you can choose to leave one later...

Chapter 2

The second chapter of the book with the title "How Your Habits Shape Your Identity (and Vice Versa)" mentions the two main reasons changing a habit is so challenging and tackles the first. Those two reasons are first "we try to change the wrong thing" and second "we try to change our habits in the wrong way". Concerning the first point, there are three levels at which change can occur, like the layers of an onion. The first layer of behavior change is "changing the outcomes". Most of the goal-setting occurs on this level of change. The second and deeper layer is "changing the processes", that's the layer most of habit-forming is associated with. The third and deepest layer is "changing your identity" which includes your worldview, self-image, beliefs, assumptions, and biases.

Change on any level is useful, but the direction of change (inward or outward) is critical to long-term change. Behavior that is incongruent with the self will not last; however, when a habit becomes part of the identity, it serves as a catalyst to stickiness. True behavior change is identity change and therefore a goal should not be stated in the words like "read a book", but rather "become a reader".

Once a person believes that a particular characteristic is part of their identity, then they act according to that belief. For example, once a person incorporates exercise into their identity, training becomes the right thing to do. This consistency, however, works both ways. Attaching to your identity beliefs like "I'm not good with technology" lead to cognitive slumber and the deeper it is attached, the harder it is to change it. Identity conflict and resisting self-image are the biggest obstacles to positive change. That's why progress requires unlearning.

Identity change comes from embodying different elements through habits. By writing every day, you embody the identity of a writer. By training every day, you embody the identity of an athletic person. The repetition that comes with a habit is proof that makes you believe that this activity is part of your identity. The process of building habits is actually the process of becoming oneself and the frequency of those micro changes leads to gradual evolution. No single instance transforms a belief. Changing your identity is a simple two-step process: decide the type of person you want to be and prove it to yourself with small wins.

This process works not only for individuals but also for teams, communities, and nations. Choosing the values and principles you stand for allows you to recognize the type of person or community you wish to become. By aspiring to be that kind of person forces you to begin taking small steps to reinforce your desired identity. This creates a feedback loop where your habits shape your identity and your identity shapes your habits. The choice of who you want to become forms your habits and gives them their most precious value, their transformative effect.

Chapter 3

Chapter 3 "How to Build Better Habits in 4 Simple Steps" opens with the description of an experiment of Edward Thorndike. Thorndike put cats in puzzle boxes that would require them to take some simple action (like pressing a lever) in order to open the door and reveal a bowl of food. The important principle that was revealed is that "behaviors followed by satisfying consequences tend to be repeated and those that produce unpleasant consequences are less likely to be repeated."

Habits serve a very specific purpose in the brain. In every new situation, the brain is called to make a decision. Processing expends energy while every decision is recorded. This creates the feedback loop of try, fail, learn, and try differently. Habits allow the brain to skip that process and create a cost-effective rule of "if this, then that". Experience creates mental shortcuts and the conscious mind pawns off tasks to the nonconscious mind. That way the limited attention of the conscious mind can be shifted to the most essential task while habits take care of the rest. Consequently, habits create freedom and the mental space needed for free-thinking and creativity. Building habits in the present allows you to do more of what you want in the future.

There are four simple and consecutive parts that make up the process of forming a new habit. They are the cue, the craving, the response and lastly the reward. The cue is a bit of information that predicts a reward and triggers the brain to initiate a behavior. A craving is the force behind each habit that motivates you. In the absence of a craving, you have no reason to act. They differ for each person because they come from the interpretation of the cues. Same cue, different interpretation. The response is the actual habit you perform, which can take the form of a thought or an action and can occur only if you're capable of doing it. Finally, the response delivers a reward, the goal of the habit, serving two purposes: satisfying your craving, and teaching the brain that these actions are worth remembering, closing the feedback loop.

The neurological feedback loop formed by those four steps is called a habit loop. This process is an endless cycle happening every moment in a split second and is divided into two phases. The first is the problem phase which includes the cue and the craving. The brain recognizes that something needs to change. The second is the solution phase and includes the response and the reward. You take action and achieve the desired change. Habits rule our lives and we hardly notice them.

The author transforms those four steps to a practical framework he calls the "Four Laws of Behavior Change". It includes four rules that each corresponds to its respective step. The first rule is "Make it obvious", the second is "Make it attractive", the third is "Make it easy" and the fourth is "Make it satisfying". Inverting the laws offers a way to break a bad habit. Replace on the aforementioned rules the words "obvious" with "invisible", "attractive" with "unattractive", "easy" with "difficult", and "satisfying" with "unsatisfying" and you have the inverted laws.

Chapter 4

The second part of the book refers to "The First Law: Make it Obvious" and starts with the fourth chapter titled "The Man Who Didn't Look Right". The author mentions a lot of stories of people who reacted automatically or came to a significant decision by a small indiscernible piece of information. A paramedic who saved her father-in-law from a serious heart attack with a single glance, a lieutenant who ordered a missile shot down and saved a battleship by distinguishing the missile from friendly planes in the radar and more.

The human brain is a predicting machine and experiencing something repeatedly allows it to react faster. Our brains and bodies are performing magnificent feats without our conscious self-participating. We don't have to be aware of a cue for a habit to begin. That's the element of habits that makes them not only useful but dangerous, too. For that reason, behavior change should start with awareness and effective identification of current habits, in the words of psychologist Carl Jung "Until you make the unconscious conscious, it will direct your life and you will call it fate."

The rest of the chapter highlights the importance of awareness and offers two strategies to effectively raise it in our daily life. The first is the Point-and-Calling strategy. This is used by the conductors in the Japanese railway system, where they will point to certain objects and call out the information. The tactic of involving multiple body parts to a repetitive process raises awareness and makes it more likely for problems to be noticed. If it's a bad habit, saying out loud the action that you're about to take and its long term effect makes the consequences more real and easier to stop. This approach is also useful because saying aloud tomorrow's actions makes it remembering it easier.

The second strategy to raise awareness is keeping a Habit Scorecard. This a simple list of your daily habits, where you write down all of the habits that you observe in the day without judgment, just the thoughts and actions. Next, you assign a "+" next to a good habit, a "-" next to a bad, and a "=" next to a neutral one. Identifying the right sign means finding out which habit is effective at getting you closer to your goal, the type of person you want to become.

Chapter 5

Chapter five is titled "The Best Way to Start a New Habit" and gives a simple strategy to do so. Research has shown that motivation has no meaningful impact on behavior. Instead, intention to implement is much more powerful, because it leverages two of the most common cues: time and location. It takes the form of "When situation X arises, I will perform response Y." This is a strategy that many policymakers are using. It is the clarity of the sentence "I will [BEHAVIOR] at [TIME] in [LOCATION]" that sweeps away foggy notions and takes away the hindrance of deciding at the moment. Specificity strengthens your commitment and protects you from things that derail progress. Knowing exactly what you want and how you are going to accomplish it won't allow anything to distract you and pull you off course. The goal is to make the time and location so obvious that you get an urge to do the right thing at the right time.

The rest of the chapter refers to "Habit Stacking: A Simple Plan to Overhaul Your Habits". The author recounts the origin story of the Diderot Effect which states that obtaining a new possession often creates a spiral of consumption that leads to additional purchases. Denis Diderot was a poor French philosopher, who managed to acquire a scarlet robe for himself. That robe led to a chain reaction of purchases. This is a common trait of human behavior, where previous actions become the cues for the next action. When building new habits, this trait can work to your advantage. Rather than pairing your new habit with a particular time and location, you pair it with a current habit. The habit stacking technique is a special form of an implementation intention and the formula is:

- After [CURRENT HABIT], I will [NEW HABIT]."

e.g.

- After I pour my cup of coffee each morning, I will meditate for one minute.

Habit stacking also allows inserting new behaviors into the middle of your routines. Overall, habit stacking allows you to create a set of simple rules that guide your future behavior. However, in order for this approach to be successful, the right cue must be selected. When and where you choose to insert a habit into your daily routine can make a big difference. Don't ask yourself to do a habit when you're likely to be occupied with something else. Your cue should also have the same frequency as your desired habit.

The author offers two ways to find the right trigger. One is to brainstorm a list of current habits using the Habits Scorecard. The other is to create two columns. One with habits you do each day without fail and one with all of the things that happen each day without fail. Searching in there for a highly specific and immediately actionable cue becomes easier.

Chapter 6

"Motivation Is Overrated; Environment Often Matters More" is the title of the sixth chapter. The author introduces us to the power the environment has over human behavior with a story at Massachusetts General Hospital in Boston. Anne Thorndike, a primary care physician, changed the "choice architecture" in the hospital cafeteria by adding water in various places and making other similar adjustments. It increased sales of bottled water and had other similar outcomes.

People often choose products, because of where they are. The environment is the invisible hand that shapes human behavior making habits context-dependent. Kurt Lewin wrote a simple equation: Behavior is a function of the Person in their Environment or $B = f(P,E)$. It has been tested in business to describe the "Suggestion Impulse Buying" phenomenon, where customers buy products because of how they are presented to them. Perception is directed by the sensory nervous system and vision is the most powerful sensory ability. A small change in what you see can lead to a big shift in what you do.

Designing the environment for success is another way to implement the first law because if the cues that spark a habit are subtle or hidden, they are easy to ignore. If you want to make a habit a big part of your life, then make the cue a big part of your environment and sprinkle triggers throughout your surroundings. If you want to practice guitar more frequently, place your guitar stand in the middle of the living room. Environment design allows you to take back control and become the architect of your life.

The cues can start very specific, but habits can be associated over time with the entire context surrounding the behavior. Our behavior is not defined by the objects in the environment but by our relationships with them. You can train yourself to link a particular habit with a particular context. Even insomnia can be battled with this tactic. The bedroom is for sleeping only, nothing else. It is easier to associate a new habit with a new context than to build a new habit in the face of competing cues. If your space is limited, divide your room into activity zones and do the same with your digital spaces. A stable environment where everything has a place and a purpose is an environment where habits can easily form.

Chapter 7

The seventh chapter of the book is titled "The Secret to Self-Control" and focuses on the inversion of the First Law of Behavior Change: make it invisible. The story of the American troop's addiction to heroin during the Vietnam War revolutionized the common beliefs about addiction. When soldiers who had been heroin users returned home, only one in ten became re-addicted. This is directly contradictory to the reverse percentage of heroin users who got addicted in their homes. After rehab 90% of them become re-addicted.

This is highly due to the environmental cues the heroin user is exposed to. The American soldiers leave behind all of the triggers that resulted in them using heroin and the radical change in the environment leads to an overnight elimination of the addiction. On the other hand, a typical drug user returns to an environment filled with cues that caused his addiction.

Research has shown that discipline isn't the solution to bad habits. Instead, people who appear to exercise tremendous self-control actually structure their lives in a way that doesn't require heroic willpower and self-control. The way to perseverance, grit, and willpower is by creating a more disciplined environment. This is consistent with the way the habit form in the brain. Once a habit has been encoded, the urge to act follows whenever the environmental cues reappear. Once a habit is formed, it can be broken, but it's unlikely to be forgotten.

Bad habits are autocatalytic: the process feeds itself, which means they foster the feelings they try to numb. You feel bad, so you eat junk food. Because you eat junk food, you feel bad. This phenomenon is called "cue-induced wanting", where an environmental stimulus creates an irresistible urge to repeat certain bad behavior. In the short-run self-control can be effective and overpower temptation; however, in the long run, it's unlikely you can muster the willpower to override your desires every time. Thus, the secret to self-control is to make the cues of your good habits obvious and to cut the bad habits off at the source. Make the cues of your bad habits invisible.

Chapter 8

The third part of the book refers to "The 2nd Law: Make It Attractive" and starts at the eighth chapter titled "How to Make a Habit Irresistible". Scientists have found out that some animals have instinctive rules that follow when they perceive certain stimuli. While this stimulus serves a purpose in their survival, it can be artificially enhanced. These exaggerated cues are called "supernormal stimulus" and are a heightened version of reality which elicit a stronger response, too.

Humans are also prone to fall for exaggerated versions of reality. The food industry takes advantage of our Paleolithic instincts and develops products with optimized orosensation and enhanced dynamic contrast. Orosensation improves the feel of food in your mouth and enhanced dynamic contrast tricks your brain with a combination of sensations to experience novel and encourage you to not stop eating. However, this tactic is not limited to the food industry. Essentially every stimulus in today's society is engineered versions of reality to appear more attractive. The trend is for rewards to become more concentrated and stimuli to become more enticing.

The craving that the stimulus produces is due to the dopamine spike it causes. Experiments on dopamine levels in mice showed that in the absence of dopamine, mice would lose their desire and wouldn't act on anything. There was a complete absence of craving; however, they still experienced pleasure.

Higher levels of dopamine led to extreme action. It turns out that habits are dopamine-driven feedback loops.

More importantly, dopamine is secreted not only when you experience pleasure, but also when you anticipate it. It is the anticipation of a reward—not the fulfillment of it—that gets us to take action. The anticipation of reward drives action, meaning it is the craving that leads to the response. Interestingly enough our brain has significantly more neurons involved in craving rewards than for enjoying them.

The last part of the chapter enriches the habit stacking strategy with temptation bundling. That is the strategy of pairing a habit that you need to acquire with one habit that you want to do. Businesses are masters of temptation bundling and forcing their customers to associate their service or product with a desirable feeling or effect. This principle can be effectively exploited in building new habits. It's more likely to find a behavior attractive, if you get to do one pleasurable thing at the same time. The implementation of the strategy follows the following formula:

- After [CURRENT HABIT], I will [HABIT I NEED].
- After [HABIT I NEED], I will [HABIT I WANT].

e.g.

- After I get my morning coffee, I will say one thing I'm grateful for that happened yesterday (need).
- After I say one thing I'm grateful for, I will read the news (want).

Are you enjoying the book so far?

If so, please help us reach more readers by taking 30 seconds to write just a few words on Amazon.

Or, you can choose to leave one later...

Chapter 9

At the start of chapter 9, the author recounts the story of Lazlo Polgar and his three daughters to highlight "The Role of Family and Friends in Shaping Your Habits". Lazlo was a firm believer that geniuses were not born but educated and trained. He attempted to prove that belief by raising his three daughters to become chess geniuses. Each girl achieved exceptional skills in chess with each younger girl being far superior from his older sister. The Polgar sisters grew up in a culture, where an obsession with chess was normal.

In many ways, human nature works like this. Humans are herd animals and one of our deepest desires is to belong. The habits of our early life are developed by imitating our family, friends, and community. Even though we follow these rules often without thinking or remembering, there are three particular groups that we draw our habits from: the close, the many, the powerful.

Our social environment has a powerful effect on our behavior. The closer we are to someone the more likely we are to imitate some of their habits and soak up their qualities and practices. Without us knowing, we are exposed to peer pressure by our friends and family, but not always in a bad way. We can leverage that trait of human nature by surrounding ourselves with people with the habits we desire to have. Specifically, to build better habits it is very effective to join a culture where your desired behavior is the normal behavior and you already have something in common with the group. Belonging to the tribe and sharing with the community your pursuit for growth and change sustains motivation. The shared identity begins to reinforce your personal identity.

Just as powerful in shaping our behavior is the influence of the many as the experiments of Solomon Ash showcase. A subject was placed in a group and was asked a simple question with an obvious answer. The rest of the group gave intentionally an incorrect answer and the subject directly opposing his own eyes and heart also delivered the incorrect answer. In the context of habit building, when changing your habits means fitting in with the tribe, change is attractive.

Once we fit in with the tribe, we wish to stand out. Respect, praise, recognition, and approval are all very strong motivators. We imitate people of high-status, power, and prestige. That is not unreasonable since these people have access to more resources, prove to be more attractive mates, and have secured their survival. Not only are we motivated to act in pursuit of those values, but we're also motivated to avoid behaviors that would lower our status.

Chapter 10

Chapter ten is titled "How to Find and Fix the Causes of Your Bad Habits" and begins with the story of a man who quit smoking. He read a book called "Allen Carr's Easy Way to Stop Smoking" which freed him from that habit. Clear explains how the author of that book systematically reframes each cue associated with smoking and gives it a new meaning. By the end of the book, the reader is convinced that smoking is the most ridiculous thing.

Every behavior has a surface level craving and a deeper, underlying motive. The author provides a short list of motives that our actions aim at fulfilling, like conserving energy or obtaining food and water. Habit-forming products and activities don't create new motivations, but rather latch onto existing motivations. They are alternate ways to address a motive and associate that specific solution with the problem. The associations formed with a habit serve the role of predicting whether the habit is worth repeating.

Life is predictive, every time our brain perceives a cue, it makes a prediction about what to do. The interpretation of the cue (and thus the association created) is determinant of the habit formed. The prediction that follows the habit leads to a craving that transforms the cue to something applicable. A craving is the sense that something is missing. The gap between your current state and your desired state provides a reason to act. Feelings are the birthplace of desire and change.

It is possible to reprogram the brain and make hard habits enjoyable with a slight mindset shift. Reframing habits to highlight their benefits instead of focusing on the hard part will make the habits more attractive. Instead of associating fatigue with exercise, associate building endurance. Instead of focusing on today's financial limitations, focus on tomorrow's financial freedom. Instead of frustrating with every interruption while meditating, view them as opportunities to practice. Instead of saying "I'm nervous" before an important event, say "I'm excited."

A very effective strategy to associate positive feelings with particular actions or behavior is to create a motivation ritual. Simply practice associating your habits with something you enjoy, then you can use that cue whenever you need a bit of motivation. The association could be achieved by doing something you enjoy just before a difficult habit and using cues that spark positive emotions to reframe the habit.

Chapter 11

The eleventh chapter of the book titled "Walk Slowly, but Never Backwards" opens the fourth part of the book referring to "The 3rd Law: Make it Easy". The author recounts a story from the University of Florida to highlight the importance of taking action. Planning, preparing, strategizing, and learning are all activities usually useful or necessary and offer the feeling of being in motion. However, being in motion doesn't produce results. To produce results and hone a skill there needs to be action.

Being in motion reassures you that you're making progress, but also helps you to avoid criticism. Without results, nobody can criticize you and you can't fail. Although planning and preparation are necessary, they should be limited and you should focus more on practicing. The first takeaway from the 3rd Law is repetition; to master a habit, you need to get your reps in, not plan it to perfection.

Habit formation is a very specific process by which a certain behavior becomes decreasingly less conscious through repetition. When the habit becomes more automatic, the efficiency is increased and the brain has clear physical changes. Each time the activity is repeated, the association becomes stronger in the brain and the connection of neurons that fire together strengthens. It doesn't matter how many days pass since a habit has been started forming, but rather the rate at which the behavior is performed. That means that the simplest and most critical step to encode a new habit is to put in your reps. Habits form based on frequency, not time, and the learning curve flattens faster with each repetition. The effort that a hard habit demands will gradually decrease and eventually turn to automatic behavior while the brain will reflect the change physically.

Chapter 12

In chapter twelve we are introduced to "The Law of Least Effort", which states that when deciding between two similar options, people will naturally gravitate toward the option that requires the least amount of work. The first example mentioned is taken out from the book "Guns, Germs, and Steel" by Jared Diamond in which he states that the shape of each continent is the result of the farmer's behavior being constrained by the amount of friction in the environment. To put it simply, farmers expanded their farms on the easiest-to-expand direction.

The same principle governs all of our decisions. We are motivated to do what is easy and avoid repeating activities that are hard and require a lot of energy. Thus the less energy a habit requires, the more likely it is to occur. And since it isn't the habit itself that we really want, but the outcome the habit delivers, each habit is in a sense an obstacle. The less friction you face, the easier it is for your stronger self to emerge.

When building a hard habit, pumping up the motivation requires a lot of effort and causes tension in your life. Reducing friction instead of overcoming it is much more efficient. The strategy of removing points of friction that sap time and energy is referred by the author as "addition by subtraction". The central idea is to create an environment where doing the right thing is as easy as possible. Much of the battle of building better habits comes down to finding ways to reduce the friction associated with our good habits and increase the friction associated with our bad ones. Businesses capitalize on removing friction not only from their products but also from the manufacturing process.

Designing your environment is very simple. You can be proactive and after each use, reset the room and clean after your last action. Organize a space for its intended purpose and prime it to make the next action easy. If, for example, you want to draw or write more, have your drawing or writing equipment on your desk, in an obvious and easy-to-reach spot. The same principle can be inverted and you can prime the environment to make bad behaviors difficult. It's easier to avoid watching television mindlessly if after every use you unplug it, take out the batteries from the remote, and move the television into the closet.

Chapter 13

Chapter 13 is titled "How to Stop Procrastinating by Using the Two-Minute Rule". The author analyzes the power our habits have in shaping our daily decisions and on making a day a productive one. Habits can be completed in seconds; however, they can also impact your actions for hours afterward by constraining the available options. The author refers to the moments that the decisions are made which deliver such outsized impact as "decisive moments". The difference between a good day and a bad day is often a few productive and healthy choices made at decisive moments. Each one is like a fork in the road, and these choices stack up throughout the day and can ultimately lead to very different outcomes. Habits are the entry point, not the endpoint.

When you see habits as entry points, then you realize that you can apply "The Two-Minute Rule" to stick with it. The rule states that when you start a new habit, it should take less than two minutes to do. Nearly every habit and large life goal can be scaled down into a two-minute behavior. For example, "Read before bed each night" becomes "Read one page." "Study for class" becomes "Open my notes."

The idea is to make the habit as easy as possible to start even if the actions that follow are challenging. You create a "gateway habit", that is a habit that works like a gentle push from the top of a slide. After the push, you're led down undisturbed to a productive streak of actions. The more you ritualize the beginning of a process, the more likely it becomes that you can slip into the state of deep focus that is required to do great things. To make sure that you show up and don't simply reject the two-minute rule as a trick, you have to always stay below the point where it feels like work. This will also reinforce the identity you want to build.

As you master the art of showing up, the first two minutes simply become a ritual at the beginning of a larger routine. Once you have standardized your habit, you can combine the two-minute rule with the strategy of habit shaping and scale back up your habit towards your ultimate goal.

Chapter 14

The fourteenth chapter is titled "How to Make Good Habits Inevitable and Bad Habits Impossible" and starts off with the story of Victor Hugo and the writing of "The Hunchback of Notre Dame". Hugo forced himself out of procrastination by having all of his clothes taken away. Constrained at home, he managed to meet his publisher's impossible deadline. Psychologists call the technique he used a "commitment device". That is a choice you make in the present that controls your actions in the future. This technique is very effective not only at making bad habits hard - a key for success -, but also at creating a future commitment that the only way to bail out costs a lot of effort or money.

John Henry Patterson opened in 1844 a small store with little competition and a steady stream of customers. However, he struggled to make money, because, as he found out, his employees were stealing from him. Since supervision was hard, he bought the first cash register. Employee theft vanished overnight. The same principle, applied to habits, is very powerful. Increase the friction associated with bad habits to the point that it's impractical to do.

There are onetime choices you can take that require a little bit of effort up front but deliver increasing value over time. They restrict bad behavior and lead to better long-term habits. Buying a better mattress or enrolling in an automatic savings plan are such choices. Automating your habits is the

~ 39 ~

ultimate way to lock in future behavior. Technology can be a powerful ally to transforming actions that were once hard, annoying, and complicated into behaviors that are easy, painless, and simple. Deleting games and social media apps on your phone are some good examples.

Technology can work the other way, too. It minimizes the effort required to act on your impulses and leads you from easy task to easy task leaving no time for more difficult and rewarding work. When working in your favor, automation can make your good habits inevitable and your bad habits impossible. Invite inevitability to your environment by making strategic onetime decisions, using the multiple commitment devices and taking advantage of technological tools.

Chapter 15

The fifth part of the book refers to "The 4th Law: Make it Satisfying" and starts in chapter 15 titled "The Cardinal Rule of Behavior Change". At the beginning of the chapter, the author recounts the story of Stephen Luby's actions against a Pakistan city's public health crisis. Luby's team managed to create in many households the habit of washing their hands regularly. They simply made the experience more satisfying, by providing premium quality soap. The positive sensory signal the soap produced made all the difference.

The Cardinal Rule of Behavior Change states that what is rewarded is repeated and what is punished is avoided. While the first three rules increase the odds that a behavior will be performed this time, the fourth law increases the odds that a behavior will be repeated next time, closing the habit loop. Pleasure teaches the brain that a certain behavior is worth remembering and repeating. Thus it is more likely to repeat a behavior when the experience is satisfying.

The human brain is wired to live in an immediate-return environment where every decision has an immediate impact. However, our society is a predominantly delayed-return environment, where you can work for years before your actions deliver the intended payoff. By nature, we are wired to value instant gratification more and forget future consequences.

This is why we are so prone to bad habits. The benefits of bad habits are in the present, while the benefits of good habits are in the future. The costs work the other way around. The costs of bad habits are in the future and the costs of good habits in the present.

Even though this knowledge is no secret, we haven't evolved to the point of valuing future rewards without conscious effort. Nonetheless, people who are better at delaying gratification enjoy a wide array of benefits. It's possible to train yourself to delay gratification but you need to work with the grain of human nature. Therefore, the Cardinal Rule of Behavior Change is updated to: what is immediately rewarded is repeated and what is immediately punished is avoided.

The best way to do this is to add a little bit of immediate pleasure to the habits that pay off in the long-run and a little bit of immediate pain to ones that don't. Good habits are all sacrifice in the beginning and you need a reason to stay on track. You have to reinforce the ending of your habit to be satisfying. Reinforcement ties your habit to an immediate reward, which makes it satisfying when you finish. This is an effective strategy for habits of avoidance. You are rewarding yourself for avoiding a bad habit or behavior. Once the short-term reward is aligned with your long-term vision, your reinforced identity will sustain the new habit.

Chapter 16

Chapter sixteen is titled "How to Stick with Good Habits Every Day" and focuses on habit tracking. The author refers to a technique called "the Paper Clip Strategy", where each time you perform a habit you move a paper from one bin to another. Such visual measures provide clear evidence of progress. And progress is satisfying.

A habit tracker is a simple way to measure whether you did a habit and the most basic format is to get a calendar and cross off each day you stick with your routine. Habit tracking is powerful because it makes the tracked behavior not only obvious and attractive but also satisfying.

It's obvious because when you record your last action, you create a trigger that can initiate your next one and provide clarity on how much work you've put in. It's attractive because progress is the most effective form of motivation. Each small win feeds your desire and motivates you to act even on bad days. It's satisfying because tracking can be its own form of reward. When a behavior feels good, it is more likely to endure. It helps to focus on the journey instead of the destination.

Nevertheless, habit tracking isn't for everyone. Tracking and measuring force you into two habits, the one you try building and the habit of tracking it. To make it easier, automate measurement, whenever possible, and focus on tracking only essential habits. Another good tactic is to record each measurement immediately after the habit occurs. Combined with the habit-stacking method, we have the formula:

- After [CURRENT HABIT], I will [TRACK MY HABIT]

e.g.

- After I finish each set at the gym, I will record it in my workout journal.

Consistency at some point will break. You'll miss your habit and break the chain. This is inevitable. However, it will matter little, if you recover quickly. The author provides this rule: never miss twice. You might miss one repetition, but next time you have to show up. Showing up is what matters - not perfectly executing the behavior - because it reaffirms your identity.

Also, measuring the right habit protects you from focusing on things that don't matter. Goodhart's Law states that when a measure becomes a target, it ceases to be a good measure. Just because you can track something, it doesn't mean it's the most important value and vice versa. Just because you can't measure something, it doesn't mean it's not important. "Nonscale victories" matter just as much. For example, the number on the scale might be stubborn, but your sex drive got a boost.

Chapter 17

The seventeenth chapter is the last chapter that refers to an individual Law of Behavior Change and is titled "How an Accountability Partner Can Change Everything". The author underscores the effectiveness of the inversion of the 4rth Law of Behavior Change, make it immediately unsatisfying, with the story of Roger Fisher. He suggested making the nuclear codes available to the President of the U.S. by forcing him to take a life with his own hands. It was rejected.

All you have to do to prevent unwanted and unhealthy behaviors to occur is to add an artificial and immediate cost to the habit and you reduce the odds of it repeating. The more local, tangible, concrete, and instant the consequence, the more likely it is to influence individual behavior. The more global, intangible, vague, and delayed the consequence, the less likely it is to influence individual behavior.

There is a straightforward way to add an immediate cost to any bad habit: create a habit contract. A habit contract is a verbal or written agreement in which you state your commitment to a particular habit and the punishment that will occur if you don't follow through. It is a great way to hold yourself accountable by adding a social cost to violating your promises. It makes the cost public and painful.

The simple act of having an accountability partner makes failing to uphold your promises even more painful. We are always trying to present our best selves to the world. When we agree to act a certain way and don't follow along, we're punished. It's a powerful motivator to know that someone else is watching whether you succeed. You don't just violate your promise to yourself, you violate your promise to others.

Chapter 18

The last part of the book is titled "Advanced Tactics: How to Go from Being Merely Good to Being Truly Great" and starts in chapter 18 "The Truth About Talent (When Genes Matter and When They Don't)". When it comes to habit change the secret to maximizing your odds for success is to choose the right field of competition. Embracing this strategy requires the acceptance of the simple truth that people are born with different abilities. Although genes do not determine your destiny, they determine your areas of opportunity. It is more likely to enjoy success in the areas you are genetically predisposed because your habits are more likely to be satisfying. Our environment determines whether our genes are suitable for success and whether we can utilize our natural talents. When the environment changes, so do the qualities that determine success.

Genes are operating beneath the surface of every behavior and habit. According to research, every personality trait has a genetic component. The most proven scientific analysis of personality traits is known as the "Big Five," which breaks them down into five spectrums of behavior. The author mentions them and offers a few examples of their biological underpinnings. Genes cannot be easily changed, they also don't solely determine your habits. Instead, they nudge towards a certain direction. When choosing habits, choose the habits that provide the most satisfaction, the behaviors that feel easier for you.

When you pick the right habit, progress is easy. Thus you're more likely to be successful, which makes the habit more satisfying. To choose the right habit you have to find and design your environment so you're at your natural best. Exploring new activities is the only way of finding your strengths. Next, you should focus on the best solution, with occasional experimenting. Even though finding the balance isn't always easy, the author suggests focusing your time on the strategy that delivers 80-90 percent of the best results and the rest to exploring.

Clear also provides a few questions to narrow in on the habits and areas that will be most satisfying to you:

- What feels like fun to me, but work to others?
- What makes me lose track of time?
- Where do I get greater returns than the average person?
- What comes naturally to me?

We all have limited time on this planet, and the truly great among us are the ones who not only work hard, but also have the good fortune to be exposed to opportunities that favor us. However, if you can't play a game that favors you, create one. Combining moderate and diverse skills create a unique advantage by reducing the level of competition. Nonetheless, genes don't eliminate the need for hard work, they clarify it. The better we understand our nature, the better our strategy can be.

Chapter 19

Chapter nineteen is titled "The Goldilocks Rule: How to Stay Motivated in Life and Work" and starts with the incredible story of Steve Martin. He spent 10 years working on his craft and another 4 in refining it before he enjoyed wild success. Martin's comedy career is an excellent example of the Goldilocks Rule in practice, which states that humans experience peak motivation when working on tasks that are right on the edge of their current abilities. Only when a challenge is of "just manageable difficulty" do we achieve peak level of desire and become fully immersed in the activity.

When the task is too easy, then we get bored. If the task is too difficult, then we lose all motivation. When you're starting a new habit, it's important to keep the behavior as easy as possible so you can stick with it even when conditions aren't perfect. Once a habit has been established, however, it's important to continue to advance in small ways. Improvement requires a delicate balance and boredom is perhaps the greatest villain on the quest for self-improvement. Behaviors need to remain novel in order for them to stay attractive and satisfying.

Sometimes it's possible to introduce novelty to a behavior with what is known as a variable reward. Applying the Goldilocks rule with a habit amplifies the craving and keeps things interesting. However, not all habits have variable rewards and you wouldn't want them to. In those cases, you have to fall in love with boredom.

The difference between professionals and amateurs is that the former stick to the schedule, while the latter let life get in the way. The only way to achieve mastery is through practice and practice gets boring pretty fast. Anyone can work hard when they feel motivated. Consistency and the ability to keep going when the work isn't exciting are what make the difference.

Chapter 20

The final chapter of the book is the twentieth chapter with the title "The Downside of Creating Good Habits". Habits create the foundations for mastery. Every activity and discipline requires mastering the essential parts before moving on the more advanced details. Although good habits and repetition develop fluency, speed, and skill, they also reduce sensitivity to feedback. You get used to doing things a certain way and stop paying attention to little errors. Habits are necessary, but not sufficient for mastery.

To maximize your potential and achieve elite levels of performance, you also need to practice deliberately. The formula is: Habits + Deliberate Practice = Mastery. Some skills do need to become automatic, but you need to progressively layer improvement on top of one another. Remain conscious of your performance over time by pouring your energy into the next challenge. To successfully master a skill and avoid slipping into the trap of complacency, you have to establish a system for reflection and review.

The head coach of the Los Angeles Lakers basketball team in 1985 Pat Riley created the Career Best Effort program or CBE. They tracked certain basketball statistics for each player that joined the team and determined his baseline level of performance. Then Riley asked each player to "improve their output by at least 1 percent over the course of the season." Riley compared each player's current CBE to not only their past performances but also those of other players in the league. However, they emphasized year-over-year progress by making historical comparisons of CBE data. Eight months after the program rolled out, Lakers were NBA champions.

The CBE program is a prime example of the power of reflection and review. It made sure their habits improved rather than declined. Reflection is an essential part of the path to mastery because it makes you aware of your mistakes and helps you consider possible paths for improvement. It is in that process that we refuse to believe in our excuses through rationalizations and the lies that occur. Improvement is not just about learning habits, it's also about fine-tuning them. Reflection and review ensures that you spend your time on the right things and make course corrections whenever necessary.

Reflection can also bring a sense of perspective by shifting the focus from the minor details to the big picture. Reflection and review offers an ideal time to revisit one of the most important aspects of behavior change: identity. The reinforcement of the new identity is accompanied by a sense of "pride" that encourages you to deny your weak spots and prevents you from truly growing. You have to keep your identity detached from your roles and flexible. Only then can you adapt to new challenges and protect yourself from an identity crisis.

The author employs two primary modes of reflection and review: an Annual Review every December and an Integrity Report every six months.

The book concludes that the holy grail of habit change is not a single 1 percent improvement, but a thousand of them. It suggests a commitment to tiny, sustainable, unrelenting improvements because success is a system to improve, an endless process to refine and not a goal to reach.

The author has also compiled "Little Lessons from the Four Laws" to clarify just how useful and wide-ranging the four-step model he introduced is when describing human behavior. Here is the list:

- Awareness comes before desire.
- Happiness is simply the absence of desire.
- It is the idea of pleasure that we chase.
- Peace occurs when you don't turn your observations into problems.
- With a big enough "why" you can overcome any "how".
- Being curious is better than being smart.
- Emotions drive behavior.
- We can only be rational and logical after we have been emotional.
- Your response tends to follow your emotions.
- Suffering drives progress.
- Your actions reveal how badly you want something.
- Reward is on the other side of sacrifice.
- Self-control is difficult because it is not satisfying.
- Our expectations determine our satisfaction.
- The pain of failure correlates to the height of expectation.
- Feelings come both before and after the behavior.
- Desire initiates. Pleasure sustains.
- Hope declines with experience and is replaced by acceptance.

Background Information about Atomic Habits

Atomic Habits: An Easy and Proven Way to Build Good Habits and Break Bad Ones by James Clear was published in October of 2018. The book has sold more than 1 million copies worldwide, been translated in more than 40 languages, and spent 15 consecutive months on the New York Times bestseller list. Clear offers a framework that is an integrated model of the cognitive and behavioral sciences. His goal was to write an operating manual about the fundamentals of human behavior and how to take advantage of them. His instructions guide the reader on how to progressively develop good habits and break bad ones with small changes in his life. It is an actionable guide on creating from within the identity you desire.

Background Information about James Clear

James Clear is a New York Times bestselling author and a speaker. He has published over 150 articles and his work on habits, decision-making, and continuous improvement has appeared in magazines such as the Entrepreneur and Time magazines the New York Times, the Wall Street Journal, and on CBS This Morning. His popular 3-2-1 weekly newsletter has over 700.000 subscribers while his website enjoys more than 10 million visitors each year. Coaches and players in the NFL, NBA, and MLB use his work and his past clients include Cisco, General Electric, Honda, Intel, LinkedIn, Lululemon, McKinsey & Company, Merrill Lynch, and many more. In his mission to "help others realize their full potential," he donates 5% of profit to Against Malaria Foundation each year. He enjoys ultralight traveling, travel photography, architecture, good restaurants, and book reading. He has personal lists of book recommendations on his website as well as transcripts of great speeches. Through the online course he has created, The Habits Academy, Clear has successfully taught more than 10,000 leaders, managers, coaches, and teachers.

Cover Questions

- How can I build a system to get 1% better every day?
- Which habits are good and which are bad?
- How do I break my bad habits and stick to good ones?
- How can I avoid the common mistakes most people make when changing habits?
- Can I overcome my lack of motivation and willpower?
- How do I develop a stronger identity and believe in myself?
- Is it possible to make time for new habits?
- Can I design my environment to make success easier?
- What tiny, easy changes can I make that deliver big results?
- How do I achieve greatness?
- I got off course, is there a way to get back on track?
- Where can I apply this framework?

Thank You

Hope you've enjoyed your reading experience.

We here at Book Tigers will always strive to deliver to you the highest quality guides.

So I'd like to thank you for supporting us and reading until the very end.

Before you go, would you mind leaving us a review on Amazon?

It will mean a lot to us and support us in creating high-quality guides for you in the future.

Thanks once again and here's where you can leave a review.

Warmly yours,

The Book Tigers Team

Download Your Free Gift

Before you go any further, why not pick up a gift from us to you?

Investing In You – Using the Power of Positive Thinking.

You will understand the true power of your positive thinking and subconscious mind and you will have absolute control over them, very fast!

Scan the QR code to get it before it expires!

Discover the Book Tigers Series

If you are enjoying reading our books, please take a moment and check our book series.

SELF HELP & SUCCES SUMMARIES

FICTION SUMMARIES

SOCIAL & POLITICS SUMMARIES

HEALTH & DIET SUMMARIES

Feel free to continue your journey with us, where you will find new resources, tools, blogs, and advance notice of new books at...

www.booksandsummaries.com

Copyright © 2020 BOOK TIGERS™

All rights reserved

Made in the USA
Coppell, TX
15 November 2021